mama says...

Eat more TORTILLAS

DONNA KELLY AND STEPHANIE ASHCRAFT

GIBBS SMITH
TO ENRICH AND INSPIRE HUMANKIND

First Edition
20 19 18 17 16   5 4 3 2 1

Published by
Gibbs Smith
P.O. Box 667
Layton, Utah 84041

1.800.835.4993 orders
www.gibbs-smith.com

Designed by Rita Sowins / Sowins Design and Virginia Snow
Corrine M. Miller: Food Stylist
Marcela Ferrinha: Food Stylist

Printed and bound in Hong Kong
Gibbs Smith books are printed on either recycled, 100% post-consumer waste,
FSC-certified papers or on paper produced from sustainable PEFC-certified forest/
controlled wood source. Learn more at www.pefc.org.

Library of Congress Cataloging-in-Publication Data

Names: Kelly, Donna, 1955- author. | Ashcraft, Stephanie, author.
Title: Eat more tortillas / Donna Kelly and Stephanie Ashcraft.
Description: First edition. | Layton, Utah : Gibbs Smith, [2016] | Includes
    index.
Identifiers: LCCN 2016000322 | ISBN 9781423644361 [hardcover]
Subjects: LCSH: Mexican American cooking. | Tortillas. | LCGFT: Cookbooks.
Classification: LCC TX715.2.S69 K46 2016 | DDC 641.5972–dc23
LC record available at http://lccn.loc.gov/2016000322

CONTENTS

INTRODUCTION

The thin, flexible flatbread we know as a tortilla began as a humble peasant food in Mexico and is now a well-loved staple in kitchens all over the world. Tortillas are traditionally used in Mexican dishes such as burritos, tacos, and quesadillas. But tortillas can be so much more.

Who doesn't love the portability that soft tortillas provide for wraps? In their soft form, tortillas also work great to make such tempting appetizers and meals as pinwheels, lasagna, crepes, and enchiladas.

When crisp, they provide the crunch for favorite dishes like nachos and tacos and can be used to create crusts, toppings, chips, and tasty sweet treats.

We welcome you to our collection of recipes that feature both classic dishes and creative new culinary adventures that you are sure to love.

Helpful hints for cooking with corn and flour tortillas:

1. Corn tortillas come in a standard 6-inch size. Generally, they must be cooked before being eaten. Heat an 8-inch or larger frying pan on the stovetop and lay a tortilla on the hot pan. With a spatula, flip the tortilla every 30–45 seconds, or until lightly toasted but bendable.

2. Flour tortillas come ready to eat in a variety of shapes and sizes. In this book, we refer to flour tortillas in three sizes: small (6–7 inch diameter, often called "taco size"); medium (8–10 inch diameter, and most common size); and large (11–14 inch diameter, often called "burrito size").

3. Flour tortillas come in a variety of thicknesses, including an extra-thick version called "gordita style." These are heavier than average flour tortillas, and are often used in recipes that require baking, such as for main dishes.

4. Flour tortillas often come in a variety of flavors, such as wheat, tomato, or spinach. These may be substituted for regular flour tortillas in any recipe, but baking times may need

to be adjusted, and the flavor will be a little different.

5. To prevent tortillas from cracking or breaking, soften them in the microwave before using. Place up to 4 tortillas at a time on a plate and cover with a paper towel. Microwave on high for 20–30 seconds, or until tortillas are soft and bendable. Keep covered with paper towel until ready to use.

6. Tortillas store well in the refrigerator for about 2 weeks, or in the freezer 2–3 months. Always store opened tortillas in an airtight container.

7. Rolling styles for tortillas vary according to each recipe. Generally, jelly-roll style means rolling the tortilla in a tight roll with both ends open. Burrito style means folding the ends in and then rolling the tortilla in a large roll, with no openings.

8. The first time you try baking a recipe, check the food 3–5 minutes before its minimum cooking time ends—each oven heats differently, so cooking time can vary.

9. For the health conscious, low-fat or light ingredients can be used in all recipes.

NEVER-FAIL FLOUR TORTILLAS

3 cups all-purpose flour
1 teaspoon salt
1 teaspoon baking powder
⅓ cup lard, melted (for vegetarian tortillas, use vegetable or canola oil)
1 cup hot water

Stir together all ingredients in a large mixing bowl. Turn onto a lightly floured surface and knead for 1 full minute. Place in an oiled bowl. Cover bowl with a large kitchen towel and let sit in a warm place for about 1 hour.

Make 12 balls of dough. Roll each ball out on a lightly floured surface to make a 10–12-inch circle. Cook on a large griddle or frying pan over medium-high heat until lightly browned on both sides. Makes 12 large tortillas.

TORTILLA GARNISHES

Tortilla matchsticks

With a pizza cutter, slice 2 medium flour tortillas into very thin matchstick pieces. Spread on a baking sheet and bake 5–6 minutes at 400 degrees. Stir. Return to oven 3–5 minutes more. Matchsticks should be crisp and golden brown. Cool. Makes 2 cups.

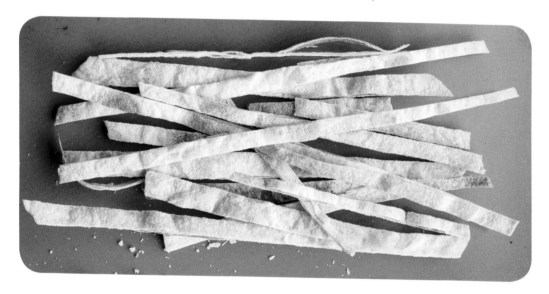

Tortilla crisps

With a pizza cutter, cut 3 corn or 2 medium flour tortillas into small rectangles. Heat canola oil in a small frying pan over medium heat. Add a small amount of tortilla rectangles to pan. They will cook quickly. Cool on a plate covered with a paper towel. Blot carefully to remove excess oil. Makes 2 cups.

Tortilla Confetti

Purchase flour tortillas of different colors at the deli section of a grocery store. With kitchen scissors or a pizza cutter, cut 2 medium tortillas into tiny squares. Use as they are, or follow Tortilla Matchsticks directions (p. 9) for crispy tortilla confetti. Makes 2 cups.

Migas (Tortilla Crumbs)

Using the leftover tortilla crumbs at the bottom of a bag of tortilla chips, crush with a rolling pin or fork. Sprinkle over main dishes, salads, or soups as an easy last-minute garnish.

APPETIZERS

SMOKED SALMON TRIANGLES

makes 24 triangles

4 tablespoons butter, divided
4 medium flour tortillas
1 (8-ounce) package cream cheese, softened
1/2 pound thinly sliced smoked salmon
2 medium tomatoes, thinly sliced
1 medium red onion, thinly sliced
1/4 cup chopped parsley or cilantro

Melt 1 tablespoon butter in a large frying pan over low heat. Cook 1 tortilla until light golden brown and crisp on one side only. Remove and cool. Repeat with remaining butter and tortillas.

Divide cream cheese into 4 equal parts and spread over each tortilla on the uncooked side. Then equally divide and top with the salmon, tomatoes, onion, and parsley or cilantro. Cut each tortilla into 6 triangle wedges. Chill before serving.

TORTILLA PINWHEELS

makes 24 pinwheels

2 (8-ounce) packages cream cheese, softened
2 tablespoons mustard
6 large flour tortillas
2 pounds thinly sliced deli turkey
4 cups chopped fresh spinach
1 red bell pepper, finely chopped
2 cups grated cheese, any type

In a small bowl, combine cream cheese and mustard. Spread ⅓ cup cream cheese mixture over each tortilla. Layer turkey, spinach, bell pepper, and cheese onto each tortilla, leaving a 1-inch border around the outside edge of the tortilla. Roll up jelly-roll style, wrap in plastic wrap, and chill at least 1 hour.

Slice each roll into 2-inch pieces and arrange on a platter. Serve chilled.

TORTILLA SUSHI ROLLS

makes 12 rolls

12 medium flour tortillas
4 tablespoons cream cheese, softened
1 cup cooked white rice
$\frac{1}{2}$ cup cooked crab meat
$\frac{1}{2}$ avocado, sliced lengthwise into 8 strips
2 tablespoons finely diced green onion or green bell pepper
$\frac{1}{2}$ cup sour cream
2 teaspoons Tabasco sauce

Trim tortillas into 6-inch squares and warm in microwave until just softened. Spread cream cheese in an even, thin layer over each tortilla. Spoon rice over half of each tortilla. Divide, and place crab meat, avocado, and green onion lengthwise over rice. Roll each tortilla up tightly, jelly-roll style and cut into 1-inch pieces. Lay pieces flat on a baking sheet. Combine sour cream and Tabasco sauce and drizzle over top. Broil 3–5 minutes, until lightly browned.

SOUTHWEST EGG ROLLS

makes 12 rolls

12 medium flour tortillas
Canola oil
2 cups shredded cabbage
2 cups chopped spinach
2 tablespoons butter
1/2 cup cooked corn kernels
1/2 cup cooked black beans
1 cup grated pepper jack cheese
1 small jar sweet-and-sour sauce

Trim tortillas into 6-inch squares and warm in microwave for 60 seconds on a plate covered with a paper towel.

Heat about 2 inches of oil in a small saucepan over medium heat. In a small frying pan, sauté cabbage and spinach in butter until just limp, not browned. Remove from heat and mix in corn, black beans, and cheese. Spread 2 tablespoons of mixture on each tortilla and roll into an egg-roll shape. Place seam-side down in hot oil in saucepan. Fry until golden brown on both sides. Serve hot with sweet-and-sour sauce for dipping.

NACHOS CON POLLO

¹/₂ cup chopped green onions
1 teaspoon minced garlic
3 tablespoons olive oil
1 (10- to 13-ounce) can chunk chicken breast, drained*
1 ¹/₂ cups chunky salsa
¹/₂ (14-ounce) bag tortilla chips
1 ¹/₂ cups grated Mexican-blend cheese

Preheat oven to 350 degrees.

In a frying pan, sauté green onions and garlic in oil until tender. Stir in chicken, shredding as you stir, and completely coat it with oil. Mix in salsa. Place tortilla chips on bottom of a baking sheet. Spoon chicken mixture evenly over chips. Sprinkle cheese over top. Bake 10 minutes, or until cheese melts. Top with more fresh green onion, if desired.

*1¹/₂ cups cooked and shredded chicken may be substituted.

SPINACH & CHEESE TRIANGLES

makes 18 Triangles

1 cup chopped green onion
$\frac{1}{2}$ cup butter, divided and melted
2 tablespoons minced garlic
$\frac{1}{4}$ teaspoon nutmeg
1 (16-ounce) bag frozen chopped spinach, thawed and drained
2 cups crumbled feta cheese or queso fresco
2 eggs, beaten
6 large, thin flour tortillas

Preheat oven to 350 degrees.

Sauté green onion in a large frying pan over medium-high heat in ¼ cup butter for 1 minute. Add garlic and nutmeg and sauté 2 minutes more. Add spinach and stir frequently until all moisture evaporates. Remove from heat and let cool to room temperature. Stir in cheese and eggs.

Cut tortillas into 3 x 10-inch strips (about 3 per tortilla). Place 2 tablespoons spinach mixture on one end of each strip, and fold into a triangle, like folding a flag. Place on wire rack on a baking sheet, seam-side down. Brush both sides of each triangle with melted butter. Bake 20 minutes, or until light golden brown.

NEVER-FAIL NACHOS

makes 3–5 servings

8 cups tortilla chips
2 cups grated cheddar cheese

Preheat oven to 475 degrees.

Spread tortilla chips on a baking sheet in a single layer. Sprinkle cheese over top. Place in oven on center rack 1–3 minutes, or until cheese melts. Remove from oven and top with desired toppings as listed below. Return pan to center of oven and broil 3–5 minutes, or until bubbly and hot.

College Survival variation: Spread 1 (16-ounce) can refried beans evenly over chips and cheese. Broil as directed above. Remove from oven and garnish with salsa, guacamole, and sour cream, if desired.

Barbecue Chicken variation: Dice 2 barbecued chicken breasts. Sprinkle over chips and cheese. Dice half of a red onion and sprinkle over top. Broil as directed above. Remove from oven, drizzle spicy barbecue sauce on top, and garnish with chopped cilantro and tomatoes.

Taco-style variation: Cook ½ pound ground beef seasoned with chili powder and garlic salt, to taste. Spoon meat on top of chips and cheese. Broil as directed above. Remove from oven and sprinkle with shredded lettuce, chopped tomatoes, and salsa.

CRANBERRY BRIE QUESADILLA BITES

makes 24 bites

6 large flour tortillas
2 pears, cored and thinly sliced
1 teaspoon lemon juice
$1/2$ teaspoon ground cinnamon
$1/4$ teaspoon ground nutmeg
$1/4$ cup dried cranberries, diced
1 tablespoon diced walnuts
4 ounces Brie cheese, thinly sliced

Cut 4 (3-inch) circles from each tortilla.

In a medium bowl, toss together the pear slices, lemon juice, cinnamon, nutmeg, cranberries, and walnuts. On half of each tortilla circle, layer 1 slice of Brie, 1 pear slice, some cranberries, and walnuts. Top with 1 more slice of Brie. Fold tortillas over and press to form half-circles.

Heat a large dry frying pan over medium heat. Place several quesadillas in the pan and cook until golden brown, 2–3 minutes per side. Repeat with the remaining quesadillas. Serve while warm.

PEPPER JELLY BITES

makes 36 bites

6 medium flour tortillas
6 tablespoons cream cheese, softened
6 tablespoons jalapeño pepper jelly
1 cup finely diced pecans

Trim each tortilla into a 6-inch square then spread with 1 tablespoon cream cheese. Spread 1 tablespoon jelly over cream cheese then sprinkle each tortilla with 2 tablespoons pecans. Roll up jelly-roll style. Wrap individually with plastic wrap and refrigerate at least 1 hour. When ready to serve, remove plastic wrap and slice into 1-inch rolls.

BREAKFASTS

OVERNIGHT BRUNCH ENCHILADAS

makes 8–10 servings

½ cup sliced green onions
¾ cup chopped green bell pepper
3 tablespoons butter, divided
16-ounces cooked cubed ham
10 medium flour tortillas
2 ½ cups grated cheddar cheese, divided
5 eggs, beaten
2 cups half-and-half
½ cup milk
1 tablespoon flour
½ teaspoon garlic powder
½ teaspoon black pepper

In a large frying pan over medium-high heat, sauté green onions and bell pepper in 1 tablespoon butter until softened. Add ham and sauté another few minutes. Spread ⅓ cup mixture down middle of each tortilla. Sprinkle 2 tablespoons cheese over top. Spread remaining butter in a 9 x 13-inch baking pan. Roll tortillas and place them, seam-side down, in pan. Mix eggs, half-and-half, milk, flour, garlic powder, and pepper together. Pour egg mixture evenly over rolled tortillas. Cover and refrigerate overnight.

Preheat oven to 350 degrees. Bake, uncovered, for 50 minutes, or until egg mixture is cooked. Sprinkle remaining cheese over enchiladas. Bake an additional 3–5 minutes to melt cheese.

HAM-AND-CHEESE BREAKFAST BURRITOS

makes 2-4 servings

³/₄ cup diced cooked ham
1 tablespoon vegetable oil
5 eggs, beaten
1 tablespoon milk
Salt and pepper, to taste
¹/₄ cup grated cheddar cheese
4 medium flour tortillas
Salsa

In a nonstick frying pan, cook ham in oil 3–4 minutes, until lightly browned. Stir in eggs and milk. Season with salt and pepper. Scramble eggs and cook over medium-low heat until done. Sprinkle cheese over eggs. Roll scrambled eggs in tortillas and serve with salsa.

GREEN CHILE
EGGS BENEDICT

makes 4 servings

2 Anaheim chile peppers
1 tablespoon vegetable oil
8 corn tortillas
4 tablespoons butter
2 cups hollandaise sauce
8 eggs
4 slices cooked ham or Canadian bacon

Remove seeds and stems from peppers and cut each pepper into 4 long strips. Toss strips in oil. Place on a baking sheet, cut sides down and broil at the top of the oven until lightly charred and softened.

In a medium frying pan, cook each tortilla in ½ tablespoon butter, turning until lightly crisp and golden brown on both sides. Place a corn tortilla on a microwave-safe plate and spread a few tablespoons of hollandaise sauce over top. Place another tortilla on top.

Poach eggs until whites are cooked through but yolks are still runny. Layer 1 slice of ham, 2 pepper strips, and 2 eggs on top of tortillas. Repeat 3 times with remaining tortillas and ingredients. Ladle ¼ cup sauce over top of each plate and heat in microwave for 30 seconds or so, until warmed through.

BREAKFAST TOSTADAS

makes 4 servings

2 tablespoons butter, softened
4 corn tortillas
1 cup grated cheddar cheese
1 ¼ cups cubed cooked ham
4 eggs, scrambled and cooked
2 cups shredded lettuce
Chopped tomato, sliced black olives, and sour cream

Preheat oven to 400 degrees.

Spread butter on one side of each tortilla and lay tortillas butter-side up on a large baking sheet. Bake 3–5 minutes, or until tortillas are toasted. Flip tortillas and sprinkle cheese over top. Bake 1–2 minutes, or until cheese melts. Remove from oven. Layer ham, scrambled eggs and lettuce over top. Garnish with tomato, olives, and sour cream, as desired.

OVERNIGHT SAUSAGE BREAKFAST CASSEROLE

makes 6–8 servings

12 eggs
3 cups milk
1 teaspoon salt
1 teaspoon dry mustard
6 medium flour tortillas, torn into small pieces
2 cups sausage, cooked and crumbled
1 cup chopped onion
$\frac{1}{2}$–1 cup chopped green bell pepper
2 cups grated cheddar or Swiss cheese

In a large bowl, whisk eggs, milk, salt, and mustard together. Pour 1 cup of egg mixture into a 9 x 13-inch baking pan that has been prepared with nonstick cooking spray. Layer half of the following ingredients in order listed: tortilla pieces, sausage, onion, bell pepper, and cheese. Cover with remaining egg mixture. Layer remaining ingredients in the same order over top, ending with cheese. Cover and refrigerate overnight.

Preheat oven to 350 degrees and bake for 40-50 minutes, or until eggs are done.

HUEVOS RANCHEROS STACKS

makes 4 servings

12 corn tortillas
4 tablespoons butter
6 cups enchilada sauce
2 cups grated cheddar cheese
8 eggs
1 cup thinly sliced green onions

In a small frying pan over medium-high heat, cook tortillas, one at a time, in a little of the butter until lightly browned and crisp. Dip tortillas in enchilada sauce to coat. Place a stack of 3 coated tortillas on each of 4 microwave-safe plates, sprinkling a little cheese between layers and on top of the stacks.

Poach or cook eggs until whites are cooked through but yolks are still runny. Place 2 cooked eggs on each stack. Drizzle on more sauce and sprinkle onions over top. Top with more cheese. Microwave each plate 60 seconds, or until hot and bubbling.

TORTILLA QUICHES

makes 6 quiches

6 small flour tortillas
Cooking oil spray
4 eggs
1 (12-ounce) can evaporated milk
1 tablespoon flour
1 teaspoon salt
1/2 cup chopped cooked ham, bacon, or sausage
1/4 cup chopped green onion
1 cup finely grated Swiss cheese
Salsa
Sour cream

Preheat oven to 350 degrees.

Place a tortilla in microwave for 20 seconds, or until softened. Spray one side of each tortilla with nonstick cooking spray and press, oiled side down, into 6 wells of a large muffin tin or 6 (10-ounce) ramekins. Tortilla will stick up about 1/2 inch over the tops.

In a small bowl, combine eggs, milk, flour, and salt; set aside.

Divide meat, green onion, and cheese into tortilla cups. Pour egg mixture over top, about 1/2 cup into each, or until about 2/3 full. Bake 50 minutes, or until set in the center and lightly browned. Remove from oven and cool slightly before serving. Serve with salsa and sour cream.

EGG-IN-THE-HOLE ENCHILADAS

makes 4 servings

4 strips bacon, diced
4 large kale leaves, stems removed, chopped into small bits
2 green onions, thinly sliced, plus more for garnish
8 ounces Monterey Jack cheese, grated
12 corn tortillas
3 tablespoons butter
2 (15-ounce) cans red enchilada sauce, warmed
4 eggs

Preheat oven to 350 degrees. In a medium frying pan, cook bacon until lightly browned. Add kale to pan and cook until softened; let cool. Toss in green onions and cheese.

Cut a hole in the center of each tortilla with a 3-inch round cookie cutter. In a small frying pan, cook the tortillas in butter on both sides until pliable, but not crisp. Spoon a little of the warmed enchilada sauce into 4 oven-safe round dishes or frying pans that are the width of the corn tortillas. (If you don't have round baking dishes, make 4 stacks of enchiladas on a baking sheet.) Place a corn tortilla on top of sauce and spoon a layer of warm sauce over top. Sprinkle generously with a layer of cheese mixture. Repeat 2 times, for a total of 3 corn tortillas in each dish. Crack an egg into the center of each dish.

Bake for 20 minutes. Check eggs and return to oven for a few minutes at a time, until egg whites are done, but yolks are soft. Garnish with a little green onion and cheese, if desired.

LAZY MORNING MIGAS

makes 6 servings

1 tablespoon butter
1 tablespoon vegetable oil
1 green bell pepper, diced
1 red bell pepper, diced
1 medium sweet onion, diced
1 jalapeño pepper, seeds removed and minced
1 small ripe tomato, diced
4 cups slightly crushed tortilla chips
12 eggs
1/4 cup milk
1 cup grated Cotija or Monterey Jack cheese
1/3 cup chopped cilantro

In a large frying pan over medium-high heat, heat the butter and oil. Add bell peppers, onion, and jalapeño and cook until softened and lightly browned, about 3–4 minutes. Add tomato and cook for another few minutes. Add tortilla chips, stirring gently to combine.

In a large bowl, whisk together the eggs and milk and pour egg mixture into frying pan. Stir gently, folding mixture as it cooks. Add cheese and cilantro; stir to combine. Serve immediately.

QUESaDILLaS
& Wraps

CRANBERRY TURKEY SPINACH WRAPS

makes 6 servings

1 cup sour cream
1 envelope ranch dressing mix
6 large burrito-size flour tortillas
1 (16-ounce) package shaved deli turkey breast slices
1 (6-ounce) bag dried cranberries
1 (6-ounce) bag spinach leaves
1 cup grated sharp cheddar cheese

In a small bowl, stir together sour cream and dressing mix. Divide and spread mixture evenly over each tortilla. Place turkey slices over top. Sprinkle 1 ounce dried cranberries down center of tortilla. Layer spinach leaves on half the tortilla. Sprinkle 2 tablespoons cheese over spinach. Roll starting with the spinach side and then wrap in plastic wrap and chill until ready to serve. Repeat with remaining tortillas.

Variation: Can be made the night before serving. One (8-ounce) container plain yogurt may be used in place of sour cream.

BLT AVOCADO WRAPS

makes 2 servings

2 medium whole-wheat tortillas
1 ripe avocado, mashed
1 tablespoon lemon juice
2 tablespoons mayonnaise
4–6 slices bacon, cooked and diced
1 cup shredded lettuce
1 medium tomato, diced

Place tortillas on plates. Mix together the avocado, lemon juice, and mayonnaise and spread over each tortilla. Divide bacon and layer in center of each tortilla. Sprinkle lettuce and tomato over top. Fold in the ends of each tortilla and roll in the sides to form a burrito-style wrap.

RANCH CALIFORNIA WRAPS

makes 4 servings

4 boneless, skinless chicken breasts, cut into strips
2 tablespoons olive oil
$^1/_2$ cup ranch dressing
4 burrito-size flour tortillas
1 avocado, peeled and cubed
2 tablespoons lime juice
1 $^1/_2$ cups shredded lettuce
1 medium tomato, chopped
$^1/_2$ cup crumbled cooked bacon pieces

In a large frying pan, cook chicken strips in oil until juices run clear. Remove from pan and chill in refrigerator.

Stir dressing into chilled chicken. Equally divide the chicken mixture and spread down the center of each tortilla. Toss avocado cubes with lime juice. Layer lettuce, tomatoes, avocado, and bacon evenly over each tortilla and roll up burrito style.

MANDARIN CHICKEN WRAPS

makes 2–4 servings

2 boneless, skinless chicken breasts
Asian seasoning or cumin, to taste
Olive or vegetable oil
Salt and pepper, to taste
4 large flour tortillas
1 (8-ounce) package cream cheese, softened
1 (8-ounce) can mandarin oranges, drained
$\frac{1}{3}$ cup thinly sliced green onion
1 cup chow mein noodles
8 red lettuce leaves

Season chicken with seasoning or cumin. In a medium frying pan, brown chicken breasts in a small amount of oil until chicken is completely cooked. Season with salt and pepper. Remove chicken from pan.

Spread cream cheese over each tortilla. Using 2 forks, shred chicken, and then divide evenly over tortillas, leaving at least 1 inch uncovered on one side. Sprinkle oranges, onion, and noodles over chicken. Lay lettuce over top. Fold in the ends of each tortilla and roll in the sides to form a burrito-style wrap. Serve immediately or wrap individually in plastic wrap and refrigerate for up to an hour until ready to serve.

ITALIAN ROAST BEEF WRAPS

makes 2 servings

2 large flour tortillas
6–8 slices roast beef
2 slices provolone cheese, cut in half
1 cup shredded lettuce
1 medium tomato, chopped
$1/4$ medium red or yellow onion, thinly sliced
2–3 tablespoons Italian salad dressing

Place tortillas on microwave-safe plates. Divide roast beef and lay over each tortilla. Place cheese halves lengthwise in the center of each tortilla. Microwave each tortilla 45–55 seconds, or until cheese melts. Divide lettuce, tomato, and onion evenly over melted cheese. Drizzle dressing over top. Fold in the ends of each tortilla then roll in the sides to form a burrito-style wrap.

TERIYAKI FISH WRAPS

makes 6–8 servings

4 (6–8 ounce) white fish fillets
1 (12-ounce) jar teriyaki marinade
2 tablespoons canola oil
3/4 cup sour cream
3/4 cup honey mustard salad dressing
8 large flour tortillas
2 cups chopped lettuce
1 medium red onion, finely diced
2 medium tomatoes, diced

Cut fish fillets into chunks, place in a bowl, and cover with teriyaki sauce. Marinate for at least 2 hours in the refrigerator.

In a large frying pan over medium-high heat, sauté fish in oil until cooked.

In a small bowl, combine sour cream and dressing. Warm tortillas in microwave. Spread dressing mixture evenly over tortillas and layer the fish, lettuce, onion, and tomatoes on one side. Fold in the ends of each tortilla and roll in the sides to form a burrito-style wrap.

Variation: Use chicken instead of fish.

TUNA MELT TRIANGLES

makes 2–3 servings

3 medium, gordita-style flour tortillas
1 (12-ounce) can tuna, drained
1 (8-ounce) package cream cheese, softened
1 cup finely grated mozzarella cheese
1/2 cup grated Parmesan cheese
1 tablespoon dried parsley
1 teaspoon lemon juice

Preheat oven to 350 degrees.

Cut each tortilla into quarters. Place triangles on a wire rack on a baking sheet or directly onto oven rack and bake 6–8 minutes. Turn triangles over and bake another 3–5 minutes, or until crisp and golden brown. Remove from oven.

In a medium bowl, mix remaining ingredients together and spread evenly over tops of tortilla triangles.

Place on a baking sheet and put on center oven rack. Broil 2–3 minutes, or until mixture is bubbly and golden brown.

OPEN-FACE PESTO QUESADILLAS

makes 2–4 servings

2 cups grated Monterey Jack cheese
4 medium flour tortillas
1 (6-ounce) jar pesto sauce
2 small tomatoes, thinly sliced
$1/2$ cup pine nuts or slivered almonds

Preheat oven to 350 degrees.

Sprinkle cheese over 2 tortillas and place remaining tortillas on top. Place in oven on a wire rack on a baking sheet or directly on rack and bake 6–8 minutes. Remove from oven and press tortilla flat with a clean dishtowel to remove any air bubbles. Turn tortillas over and bake 3–5 minutes more. Remove from oven.

Layer pesto sauce, tomatoes, and nuts over both of the tortilla stacks. Broil in oven until hot and bubbly.

CHICKEN VEGGIE QUESADILLA STACKS

makes 4 servings

1 red bell pepper
2 tablespoons vegetable oil
1 (16-ounce) container sour cream
3 cups cooked shredded chicken
2 cups grated zucchini
2 cups grated green bell pepper
6 tablespoons butter, divided
8 medium flour tortillas
2 cups grated Monterey Jack cheese
Sour cream
Salsa

Preheat oven to 450 degrees. Cut red bell pepper in quarters and toss in oil. Place on a baking sheet, cut side down. Bake for about 20 minutes at top of oven, or until pepper is lightly browned. Purée red bell pepper and sour cream in a blender. In a large frying pan, sauté chicken, zucchini, and green bell pepper in 2 tablespoons butter. Cook 5 minutes, or until vegetables are tender. Remove from heat and drain excess liquid. Add sour cream sauce.

Place 2 tortillas on a baking sheet. Spread ½ tablespoon butter on each tortilla and ladle ⅔ cup chicken mixture over top, spreading to the edges. Sprinkle with ¼ cup cheese. Repeat 3 more times, ending with cheese on top. Bake 15–20 minutes, until hot and bubbly. Cut each tortilla stack into 4 wedges. Serve with a dollop of sour cream and salsa.

CHICKEN FAJITA QUESADILLAS

makes 8–10 servings

2 tablespoons olive oil
1 pound boneless, skinless chicken breasts, cubed
1 envelope fajita seasoning mix
2 tablespoons water
1 red bell pepper, seeded and cut into bite-size pieces
2 green bell peppers, seeded and cut into bite-size pieces
1 red onion, thinly sliced
10 burrito-size flour tortillas
1 1/2 cups grated cheddar cheese
1 1/2 cups grated Mexican-blend cheese

Preheat oven to 350 degrees.

In a large saucepan, heat oil. Stir in chicken and cook until no longer pink, stirring frequently. Add seasoning mix, water, bell peppers, and onion; cook 7–8 minutes, or until vegetables are tender. Layer half of each tortilla with cheddar cheese, chicken mixture, and Mexican-blend cheese. Fold tortillas in half over meat and cheese and place on baking sheets. Bake 8–10 minutes, or until cheese melts.

SOUPS & SALADS

DO-IT-YOURSELF TORTILLA SOUP

makes 4-6 servings

12 cups hot chicken broth
3 cups 1-inch cubes cooked chicken
3 cups grated cheddar cheese
4 cups finely chopped raw vegetables, such as avocado, onion,
     green bell peppers, tomatoes, and olives
Salsa for garnish, if desired
Sour cream for garnish, if desired
1 cup Tortilla Matchsticks (p. 9)

Keep chicken broth simmering in a pan on the stove or in a slow cooker over high heat. Place each of the remaining ingredients in separate serving bowls. Let each person fill an empty soup bowl with ingredients of his or her choice. Ladle hot broth over top of ingredients and stir. Serve with a dollop of salsa or sour cream, if desired. Top with Tortilla Matchsticks.

CHICKEN ENCHILADA SOUP

makes 4–6 servings

2 cups chopped chicken breast
1 tablespoon butter
$\frac{1}{2}$ cup diced green onion
1 tablespoon minced garlic
3 cups chicken broth
1 (14-ounce) can enchilada sauce
4 corn tortillas
1 cup sour cream
2 cups grated cheddar cheese
Crushed tortilla chips

Sauté chicken in butter in a large stockpot until chicken is cooked through, about 5 minutes. Add onion and garlic and cook another few minutes, until tender. Add broth and enchilada sauce.

Cut tortillas into small pieces with a pizza cutter. Add to soup. Simmer 5–10 minutes. Add sour cream and cheese and stir until melted. Serve hot with crushed tortilla chips as a garnish.

GREEN CHILE TOMATILLO SOUP

makes 4 servings

4 tomatillos, husks removed, chopped
1 tablespoon olive oil
1 (26-ounce) can condensed chicken and rice soup
2 cups water
1 (10-ounce) can diced tomatoes with green chiles, with liquid
2 cups crushed tortilla chips
1 cup grated cheddar cheese or pepper jack cheese

Toss the tomatillos in oil and spread in a single layer on a baking sheet. Broil for 3–5 minutes at top of oven, until lightly browned. Place tomatillos in a large stock pot. Stir in soup, water, and tomatoes. Bring to a boil and remove from heat. Place tortilla chips in bottom of individual soup bowls. Pour soup over chips and sprinkle cheese over top.

ZESTY RANCH BEAN TORTILLA SOUP

makes 8–10 servings

4 boneless, skinless chicken breasts, cut into 1-inch cubes
1 medium onion, diced
2 tablespoons vegetable oil
4 cups low sodium chicken broth
1 (15-ounce) can kidney beans, drained
1 (15-ounce) can garbanzo beans, drained
1 (15-ounce) can ranch-style pinto beans, with liquid
1 (15-ounce) can black beans, rinsed and drained
2 (10-ounce) cans diced tomatoes with green chiles, with liquid
1 envelope taco seasoning
1 envelope ranch dressing mix
4 cups crushed tortilla chips
Grated Monterey Jack cheese
Sour cream

In a 4-quart stock pot or Dutch oven, sauté chicken and onion in oil until chicken is cooked through and lightly browned. Stir in broth, beans, tomatoes, taco seasoning, and ranch dressing mix. Simmer 20 minutes over medium-low heat, or until heated through. Serve soup over crushed tortilla chips. Garnish each bowl with cheese and a dollop of sour cream.

FESTIVE CONFETTI SALAD

makes 4 servings

1 (16-ounce) container cottage cheese
¼ cup diced carrot
¼ cup diced onion
¼ cup diced red bell pepper
¼ cup diced green bell pepper
1 (8-ounce) can pineapple tidbits, drained
1 teaspoon sugar or sweetener, to taste if needed
6 cups blue corn tortilla chips
½ cup toasted sunflower seeds

Place cottage cheese in a strainer and press lightly to remove most of the liquid. In a medium bowl, mix together cottage cheese, vegetables, pineapple, and sugar. Spread a handful of tortilla chips around edges of 4 salad plates. Top each plate with 1 cup mounded cottage cheese mixture in center of the plate. Sprinkle generously with sunflower seeds. Eat, using tortillas as scoops.

CHICKEN FAJITA SALAD

makes 4-6 servings

1 pound boneless, skinless chicken breasts, cubed
1 envelope fajita seasoning
1 (10-ounce) bag romaine lettuce
1 red bell pepper, diced
1 green bell pepper, diced
$^1/_2$–1 red onion, thinly sliced
1–2 limes, quartered
1 cup grated cheddar or pepper jack cheese
Tortilla chips, crushed
Ranch dressing
Salsa

Place chicken in a large ziplock bag. Marinate in fajita seasoning according to package directions.

In a large frying pan, sauté chicken until done. Equally divide lettuce on individual plates, and then evenly sprinkle bell peppers and onion over lettuce. Layer cooked chicken over top. Squeeze lime juice over each salad. Sprinkle cheese and tortilla chips over top. Serve with ranch dressing and salsa on the side.

Variation: Layer 1 (15-ounce) can of drained and rinsed black beans over lettuce before chicken is added.

SEAFOOD TOSTADA SALAD

makes 6 servings

8 ounces tiny shrimp, cooked and chilled
8 ounces crab meat, cooked and chilled
1 ripe avocado, diced
1 green onion, thinly sliced
$1/2$ cup frozen peas
$1/4$ cup white wine vinegar
3 tablespoons canola oil
1 tablespoon sugar
6 corn tostada shells
1 (16-ounce) can refried beans, heated
2 cups grated cheddar cheese
8 cups finely chopped lettuce

In a large bowl, mix first 8 ingredients together and set aside. Spread each tostada shell with $1/4$ cup refried beans and top with $1/3$ cup cheese. Place each tostada on a plate. Stir lettuce into seafood mixture, divide into 6 servings, and mound lettuce mixture onto each tostada.

FIESTA SALAD TORTILLA CUPS

makes 6 servings

6 small flour tortillas
Cooking oil spray
1 cup corn kernels
1 can (15 ounces) black beans, drained and rinsed
3 green onions, thinly sliced
1 medium ripe tomato, diced
2 ripe avocados, diced
3 tablespoons lime juice
¼ cup extra virgin olive oil
1 clove garlic
1 tablespoon honey
1 tablespoon mayonnaise
2 tablespoons chopped cilantro, plus extra for garnish

Preheat oven to 425 degrees.

Soften the tortillas in microwave oven until pliable, but not crisp. Spray tortillas on both sides with cooking oil. Turn a large muffin tin upside down and then press oiled tortillas around 6 muffin wells, forming a bowl shape. Place on a baking sheet and bake for 8–10 minutes, until lightly browned.

In a medium bowl, combine the corn, beans, green onions, tomato, and avocados. In a blender, blend the lime juice, oil, garlic, honey, mayonnaise, and cilantro. Pour the dressing in the bowl and toss.

Spoon the salad into the baked tortilla cups and serve, garnished with cilantro.

TACO SALAD IN A TORTILLA BOWL

makes 6 servings

6 large flour tortillas
1 pound ground beef or turkey
1 tablespoon chili powder
1 teaspoon garlic salt
1 (30-ounce) can refried beans, heated
6–8 cups shredded lettuce
3 cups chopped tomatoes
3 cups grated cheddar cheese
Salsa

Preheat oven to 375 degrees.

Spray an empty 4- to 5-inch-diameter can placed on a baking pan with nonstick cooking spray. Drape a tortilla over top. Bake 8–10 minutes, or until light golden brown. Let cool 5 minutes before removing tortilla from can. Repeat with remaining tortillas.

In a large frying pan, add ground beef and spices and cook until browned, breaking into small pieces. Drain grease. Place tortilla bowls on plates. Spread beans evenly in bottom of each tortilla bowl, spoon meat over beans, and layer remaining ingredients over top of meat.

NOTE: to simplify this recipe, substitute ready-made tortilla bowls.

main
dishes

MUSHROOM SWISS TORTILLA BAKE

makes 6–8 servings

1 pound mushrooms, sliced ¼ inch thick
1 cup chopped green onions
½ cup butter
1 (19-ounce) can enchilada sauce
1 (15-ounce) can black beans, with liquid
12 corn tortillas
1 pound Swiss cheese, grated
Sour cream
Salsa

Preheat oven to 350 degrees.

In a medium frying pan, sauté mushrooms and onions in butter until limp. Blend enchilada sauce and black beans in blender until smooth. Pour a little sauce in the bottom of a 9 x 13-inch pan. Place 6 tortillas in bottom of pan. Spread half of mushroom and onion mixture in pan over tortillas. Pour half of sauce in pan, and sprinkle half of cheese over top. Repeat layers with remaining ingredients. Bake 40 minutes or until bubbly. Serve with a dollop of sour cream and salsa.

FAMILY FAVORITE TACO CASSEROLE

makes 6–8 servings

1 pound lean ground beef
1 medium onion, finely chopped
2 (8-ounce) cans tomato sauce
1 envelope taco seasoning
10 medium flour tortillas
1 (10.5-ounce) can condensed cream of chicken soup
¾ cup milk
2 cups grated cheddar or Mexican-blend cheese

Preheat oven to 350 degrees.

In a large frying pan, brown beef and onion together until meat is done and onion is translucent. Drain any excess liquid. Stir tomato sauce and taco seasoning into meat mixture.

Line bottom and sides of a buttered 9 x 13-inch pan with 6 tortillas. Spread beef mixture over tortilla crust. Place remaining tortillas over top, cutting to fit if necessary, and covering completely. Mix together soup and milk, and pour over tortillas. Sprinkle cheese over top. Cover with aluminum foil and bake 15 minutes. Uncover and bake an additional 5 minutes, or until cheese is completely melted.

NOTE: Casserole can be assembled the night before and stored in the refrigerator until 10 minutes prior to baking.

SOUTHWEST LASAGNA

makes 8-10 servings

1 (15-ounce) container ricotta cheese
1 (10-ounce) package frozen chopped spinach, thawed and pressed dry
1 pound lean ground beef
8 ounces ground Mexican chorizo, uncooked without casings
9 medium flour tortillas, torn into small pieces
1 (19-ounce) can enchilada sauce, mixed with 1 cup salsa
1 cup sliced black olives
$1/2$ pound grated mozzarella cheese
1 cup grated Parmesan cheese

Preheat oven to 350 degrees.

Prepare a 9 x 13-inch pan with nonstick cooking spray. In a medium bowl, mix together the ricotta cheese and spinach until well combined.

In a large frying pan over medium-high heat, cook ground beef and chorizo until lightly browned, about 5–8 minutes, breaking into small bits as you cook. Drain excess liquid from pan.

Layer $1/3$ of each ingredient, starting with tortillas, and then ricotta cheese mixture, enchilada sauce mixture, olives, hamburger mixture, and mozzarella. Repeat layers 2 more times. Sprinkle Parmesan over top. Bake 40–50 minutes, or until bubbly.

CHICKEN TAQUITOS

makes 4–6 servings

4 cups cooked diced chicken
1 (8-ounce) package cream cheese
1 (4-ounce) can diced green chiles, with liquid
1 teaspoon seasoned salt
8 medium gordita-style flour tortillas
¼ cup butter, melted
Guacamole
Salsa

Preheat oven to 350 degrees.

In a large bowl, mix together the chicken, cream cheese, chiles, and salt. Soften a tortilla in microwave for 20 seconds. Place ½ cup chicken mixture in a line down the center of the tortilla. Fold in the ends of tortilla then roll the sides burrito style. Place seam side down in a 9 x 13-inch pan that has been prepared with nonstick cooking spray. Repeat for each tortilla. Brush each roll with melted butter. Bake 30 minutes, or until golden brown. Garnish with guacamole or salsa, as desired.

STACKED BLACK BEAN TORTILLA PIE

makes 4-5 servings

1 (16-ounce) can refried beans
1 cup salsa, divided
1 teaspoon minced garlic
1 tablespoon dried cilantro
1 (15-ounce) can black beans, rinsed and drained
1 medium tomato, chopped
7 medium flour tortillas
2 cups grated cheddar cheese
Salsa
Sour cream

Preheat oven to 400 degrees.

In a small bowl, combine the refried beans, 3/4 cup salsa, and garlic. In a separate bowl, combine the remaining salsa, cilantro, black beans, and tomato. Place a tortilla in the bottom of a pie pan that has been prepared with nonstick cooking spray. Spread 1/4 of the refried bean mixture over tortilla within 1/2 inch of the edge. Sprinkle 1/4 cup cheese over beans and cover with another tortilla. Spoon 1/3 of the black bean mixture over top. Sprinkle 1/4 cup cheese over black bean mixture, and cover with another tortilla. Repeat layers, ending with a final layer of refried bean mixture spread over the last tortilla. Sprinkle with 1/2 cup cheese. Cover with aluminum foil and bake for 35-40 minutes. Serve individual pieces of pie with salsa and sour cream.

SLOW COOKER BURRITO CASSEROLE

makes 8 servings

1 pound lean ground beef
1 envelope taco seasoning
1 medium onion, diced
1 green bell pepper, diced
1 (15-ounce) can black beans, drained and rinsed
1 (15-ounce) can ranch-style pinto beans, with liquid
2 (10-ounce) cans tomatoes and green chiles, drained
10 medium flour tortillas, torn into pieces
4 cups grated cheddar cheese

Brown ground beef in a large frying pan over medium-high heat. Stir in taco seasoning, onion, and bell pepper and cook until vegetables are softened, about 3–5 minutes.

Evenly layer 1/3 of each ingredient starting with seasoned ground beef in the order listed above in a 4½- to 6-quart slow cooker that has been prepared with nonstick cooking spray. Repeat layers twice more. Cover and cook for 6–8 hours on low heat or 3–4 hours on high heat.

TEX-MEX MEATLOAF

makes 6–8 servings

2 eggs, lightly beaten
8 corn tortillas, pulverized in food processor
¼ cup minced onion
1 (4-ounce) can diced green chiles, with liquid
1 tablespoon chili powder
1 teaspoon salt
2 pounds lean ground beef

sauce

1 cup ketchup
2 teaspoons chili powder
¼ cup brown sugar
1 tablespoon apple cider vinegar

Preheat oven to 350 degrees.

In a large bowl, mix together the eggs, corn tortilla bits, onion, chiles, chili powder, salt, and ground beef until well combined. Shape into 2 small loaves and place in a 9 x 13-inch pan. Bake 40 minutes.

While loaves are baking, place the ketchup, chili powder, brown sugar, and vinegar in a small saucepan; bring to a simmer and cook until thickened, about 3 minutes. Remove loaves from oven and spread sauce over tops. Bake for another 20 minutes.

TORTILLA-CRUSTED FISH FILLETS

makes 4 servings

1 egg mixed with 1 tablespoon water
1 cup seasoned bread crumbs
1 cup finely crushed tortilla chips
4 (4-ounce) white fish fillets, of choice
2 tablespoons butter

Preheat oven to 400 degrees.

Place egg mixture, crumbs, and tortilla chips in separate bowls or plates. Dip fish fillets, one at a time, in egg mixture, bread crumbs, and then in crushed tortilla chips, in that order. Sauté each fish fillet in butter in an oven-safe frying pan over medium-high heat for 1 minute on each side. Place frying pan in oven and bake fillets for 5 minutes. Begin checking every 2–3 minutes and bake until fillets are cooked through and opaque. Cooking time will vary according to thickness of fillets.

GREEN CHILE TURKEY TORTILLA CASSEROLE

makes 6-8 servings

3 cups chopped cooked turkey
1 (4 ounce) can diced green chiles, with liquid
³/₄ cup chicken broth
2 (10.75-ounce) cans condensed cream of chicken soup
1 medium onion, chopped
8–10 medium gordita-style flour tortillas
2 cups grated Monterey Jack cheese, divided

Preheat oven to 350 degrees.

In a large bowl, combine the turkey, chiles, broth, soup, and onion. Prepare a 9 x 13-inch pan with nonstick cooking spray and cover the bottom with half of the tortillas. Spread half the turkey mixture over the tortilla layer. Sprinkle half the cheese over top. Repeat layers. Bake for 25–30 minutes, or until bubbly and heated through.

TORTILLA BEEF CANNELLONI

makes 4-6 servings

1 (24-ounce) jar spaghetti sauce
1 pound lean ground beef
1 teaspoon garlic salt
1 tablespoon Italian seasoning
1 cup grated mozzarella cheese
12 medium flour tortillas
Grated Parmesan cheese

Preheat oven to 375 degrees.

Spread 3 tablespoons of spaghetti sauce in the bottom of a 9 x 13-inch pan. In a large frying pan over medium-high heat, brown the ground beef and drain excess liquid; add garlic salt, Italian seasoning, and mozzarella cheese.

Trim tortillas into 6-inch squares. Place 2 tablespoons beef along one edge of a tortilla square. Roll up, jelly-roll style, and place seam side down in pan. Repeat process with each tortilla square. Pour remaining sauce over top. Bake 30 minutes. Garnish with Parmesan cheese.

FAJITA BURGER WRAPS

makes 6 servings

6 tablespoons canola oil
1 tablespoon chili powder
1 teaspoon white pepper, optional
6 medium flour tortillas
6 (¼-pound) ground beef patties
2 cups sliced red, green, and/or yellow bell peppers
6 leaves lettuce
1 large tomato, sliced
6 slices cheddar or pepper jack cheese

Heat a large frying pan or outdoor grill. Mix oil and spices in a small dish. Brush one side of each tortilla with oil mixture. Sauté or grill each tortilla until slightly crisp but not hard, about 30 seconds on each side. Cook or grill patties until done to liking. Cut them in half and set aside. Sauté or grill sliced peppers until just cooked, not limp.

To assemble burger, place 2 halves of patties lengthwise down the center of a tortilla. Add some peppers, lettuce, tomato, and cheese over top. Fold tortilla in half to form a giant taco-looking burger.

Variation: Substitute a chicken breast or veggie burger patty for the ground beef.

TORTILLA SPINACH & CHEESE CANNELLONI

makes 6 servings

1 (16-ounce) jar Alfredo sauce
1 (10-ounce) package frozen chopped spinach
1 tablespoon vegetable oil
1 teaspoon garlic salt
1 tablespoon Italian seasoning
1 cup grated mozzarella cheese
1 cup ricotta cheese
12 medium flour tortillas
Parmesan cheese, for garnish

Preheat oven to 375 degrees.

Prepare a 9 x 13-inch pan with nonstick cooking spray and spread 3 tablespoons Alfredo sauce evenly over bottom.

In a large frying pan, sauté spinach in oil over medium-high heat until just wilted, about 3 minutes. Stir in garlic salt, Italian seasoning, mozzarella, and ricotta cheeses. Trim tortillas into 6-inch squares. Place 3 tablespoons mixture along one edge of a tortilla square. Roll up and place seam side down in pan. Repeat for each tortilla square. Pour remaining sauce over tortillas. Bake 30 minutes. Garnish with Parmesan cheese.

MOM'S WHITE ENCHILADAS

makes 6 servings

¼ **cup flour**
½ **cup butter, divided**
3 cups chicken broth
1 (12-ounce) can diced green chiles
1 (16-ounce) container sour cream
12 corn tortillas
Butter
1 pound grated Monterey Jack cheese
6–8 green onions, chopped
Diced tomatoes

Preheat oven to 350 degrees.

In a large frying pan, cook flour in ¼ cup butter until golden brown; add broth and stir until smooth. Cook over medium heat until thickened, about 5 minutes. Remove from heat and stir in green chiles and sour cream. Spread 1 cup of sauce in bottom of a 9 x 13-inch pan and set the rest aside to cool.

In a separate frying pan, cook tortillas, one at a time, in remaining butter until firm but not crisp. Place ⅓ cup cheese and 1 tablespoon green onions on each tortilla and roll, jelly-roll style. Place rolled tortillas seam side down in pan. Pour remaining sauce over top. Bake 40–50 minutes, or until bubbly. Serve warm with tomatoes and green onions.

VEGETARIAN TACO CASSEROLE

makes 6 servings

1 (15-ounce) can black beans, drained and rinsed
1 (15-ounce) can ranch-style pinto beans, with liquid
1 cup salsa
$1/2$ cup sour cream
2 green onions, thinly sliced
2 teaspoons chili powder
3 cups crushed tortilla chips
2 cups grated cheddar cheese
2 cups shredded lettuce
1 medium tomato, chopped

Preheat oven to 350 degrees.

In a medium bowl, mix together the beans, salsa, sour cream, green onions, and chili powder. Layer half of bean mixture, chips, and cheese in that order in an 8 x 10-inch pan. Repeat layers. Bake 20–30 minutes, or until bubbly. Serve topped with lettuce and tomato.

GREEN CHILE PORK BURRITOS

makes 6–8 servings

2 pounds lean boneless pork roast, cut into 2-inch cubes
2 tablespoons minced garlic
1 (10-ounce) can tomatoes and green chiles, with liquid
1 (4-ounce) can chopped green chiles
Chili powder and salt, to taste
8 medium flour tortillas
Guacamole
Sour cream
Salsa

Place pork and garlic in a 4½- to 6-quart slow cooker that has been prepared with nonstick cooking spray. Cover and cook on low heat for 8–10 hours, or on high heat 4–6 hours. When tender, pull pork apart using 2 forks. Add tomatoes and green chiles and cook 1 hour more on high, uncovered. Season with chili powder and salt.

Place about ½ cup mixture on each tortilla, roll up, and serve. Garnish with guacamole, sour cream, and salsa.

FLANK STEAK FAJITAS

makes 6 servings

¼ cup lime juice
1 tablespoon soy sauce
1 tablespoon olive oil
1 tablespoon minced garlic
1 teaspoon white pepper
1 pound flank steak
¼ cup canola oil
1 yellow or purple onion, cut into ¼-inch strips
1 each red, green, and yellow bell pepper, cut into ¼-inch strips
12 medium flour tortillas

In a small bowl, mix together the first 5 ingredients. Pour mixture over steak and marinate in refrigerator, covered, at least 4 hours or overnight.

Remove steak from refrigerator and let come to room temperature, about 30 minutes. Grill or broil steak until lightly charred on both sides and medium-rare inside. Set aside and let it rest at least 10 minutes. Slice rested steak across the grain into ¼-inch slices.

Heat oil in a large frying pan until very hot. Add onion and bell peppers. Sauté until vegetables are cooked through but not limp. Turn off the heat and stir in steak strips. While frying pan mixture is still sizzling, serve with flour tortillas.

Variations: Most meats and vegetables are excellent cooked in the same style as directed above. Possible combinations are shrimp or white fish fillets with mushrooms and onion, chicken strips with zucchini, or veggie fajitas with a variety of vegetables.

DOUBLE-DECKER TACOS

makes 6 tacos

1 pound ground beef
1 envelope taco seasoning
1 (10-ounce) can diced tomatoes and green chiles, with liquid
1 (16-ounce) can refried beans
6 small flour tortillas
6 hard taco shells
1 ¼ cups grated cheddar cheese
1 ½ cups shredded lettuce
Salsa
Sour cream

In a large frying pan over medium-high heat, brown ground beef and drain excess liquid. Stir in taco seasoning and tomatoes and cook for about 10 minutes, until liquid is almost gone.

Place the refried beans in a microwave-safe bowl and heat in microwave until softened, about 90 seconds. Spread refried beans on flour tortillas. Place a taco shell on each bean-coated flour tortilla, and fold flour tortilla around outside of hard taco shell. Place a scoop of meat mixture into each taco shell. Sprinkle a small amount of cheese over meat, then add shredded lettuce over top. Garnish with salsa and sour cream.

TORTILLAS IN BLACK BEAN SAUCE

makes 6 servings

1 (15-ounce) can black beans, rinsed and drained
1 (19-ounce) can enchilada sauce
18 corn tortillas
$\frac{1}{2}$ cup butter
1 cup crumbled queso fresco cheese
1 cup chopped cilantro
2 medium tomatoes, chopped

Blend beans and enchilada sauce in blender until smooth. In a medium frying pan, sauté each tortilla in a little butter until firm but not crisp. Spread tortillas, one at a time, with black bean sauce on one side. Fold in half and then in half again. Arrange 3 folded tortilla triangles on the center of each microwave-safe serving plate. Drizzle tortillas with more sauce. Microwave on high for 1½–3 minutes, or until heated through. Serve topped with a little queso fresco, cilantro, and tomatoes.

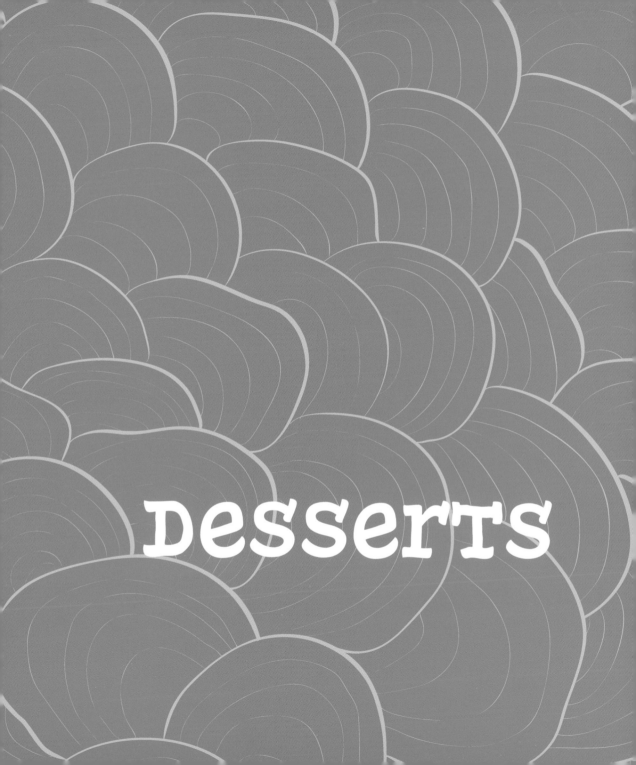

Desserts

CHERRY ENCHILADAS

makes 6 servings

1 (21-ounce) can cherry pie filling
6 medium flour tortillas
$\frac{1}{2}$ cup butter
$\frac{1}{2}$ cup sugar
$\frac{1}{2}$ cup brown sugar
$\frac{1}{2}$ cup water

Preheat oven to 350 degrees.

Spread pie filling evenly down the centers of tortillas. Fold both ends over filling then roll up jelly-roll style to form enchiladas. Place seam-side down in an 8 x 8-inch square pan that has been prepared with nonstick cooking spray.

In a medium saucepan, melt butter. Add sugar, brown sugar, and water. Stirring constantly, bring mixture to a boil. Reduce to medium-low heat and simmer 2–3 minutes. Pour sauce over enchiladas. Let the sauce cool to room temperature before baking enchiladas. Bake 15–20 minutes, or until light golden brown. Serve warm with a scoop of vanilla ice cream.

Variation: Any flavor pie filling may be substituted.

BANANA QUESADILLAS

1 (8-ounce) package cream cheese, softened
$\frac{1}{2}$ cup sugar
1 teaspoon vanilla
4 bananas
8 medium flour tortillas
Cinnamon sugar
Whipped topping
Caramel sauce
Chocolate sauce

In a small bowl, mix together the cream cheese, sugar, and vanilla until well combined. Mash 2 bananas and stir into cream cheese mixture. Spread $\frac{1}{2}$ cup banana mixture on half of a tortilla. Place tortilla in a nonstick frying pan over medium-low heat. Slice remaining bananas and add 5–6 slices over top of banana mixture. Fold plain half of tortilla over top, forming a half circle. Cook, turning about every 30 seconds until tortilla is light golden brown on both sides. Serve warm with cinnamon sugar, whipped topping, or caramel and chocolate sauce over top.

TORTILLA CANNOLIS

makes 4–6 servings

Canola oil for deep frying
8 medium flour tortillas
$1/3$ cup sugar, mixed with 2 teaspoons cinnamon
1 cup ricotta cheese
1 cup sugar-free chunky fruit jam or fresh puréed fruit
$1/2$ cup mini chocolate chips
Whipped topping

Heat about 2 inches of oil in a small frying pan or in a deep fryer to 350 degrees. Roll up a flour tortilla into a tube shape, leaving a hollow center, and fasten with a toothpick. Deep fry until golden brown. Remove from heat and, using tongs, roll immediately in sugar mixture. Repeat with remaining tortillas.

In a small bowl, mix ricotta cheese, jam, and chocolate chips together until well combined.

Fill tortilla shells with cheese mixture. Place on serving plate, and top with a dollop of whipped topping.

MEXICAN APPLE STRUDEL

makes 6–8 servings

6 cups peeled and grated cooking apples, such as Granny Smith
1 cup golden raisins
1 tablespoon lemon juice
1 tablespoon cornstarch
1 cup sugar
1 tablespoon cinnamon
1 cup chopped walnuts or pecans
8 large flour tortillas
1/2 cup butter, melted
Whipped topping

Preheat oven to 350 degrees.

In a large bowl, mix together the apples, raisins, lemon juice, cornstarch, sugar, cinnamon, and nuts.

Place tortillas, one at a time, in the microwave for about 20 seconds to soften. Spread 1 cup apple mixture on each tortilla and roll up jelly-roll style. Wrap filled tortillas tightly with plastic wrap and chill 1 hour.

Remove plastic wrap and cut tortilla rolls into 1½-inch slices. Place slices on a baking sheet and secure with toothpicks. Brush generously with butter. Bake for 30 minutes, until bubbly and golden brown. Serve with a dollop of whipped topping, if desired.

HOT FUDGE TOSTADAS

makes 4 servings

4 medium gordita-style flour tortillas
Cinnamon and sugar, to taste
6 cups vanilla ice cream, divided
1 jar hot fudge ice cream topping
Sliced fresh strawberries

Place 1 tortilla in the center of a microwave-safe cereal bowl and press down to form the shape of the bowl. Microwave for 30 seconds. Remove and press down air pockets that have formed. Microwave an additional 30 seconds. Remove tortilla and place on a tray where it can dry out. Repeat process for remaining tortillas. Sprinkle cinnamon and sugar inside bottom of tortilla bowls. Place 2–3 scoops of ice cream in each bowl. Heat hot fudge according to directions and drizzle over ice cream. Garnish with sliced strawberries

STRAWBERRY MARGARITA BITES

makes 10–12 servings

1 ½ cups finely crushed tortilla chips
¼ cup melted butter
2 tablespoons sugar
1 (14-ounce) can sweetened condensed milk
2 cups puréed strawberries
½ cup lime juice
1 (8-ounce) container frozen whipped topping, thawed
Sliced fresh strawberries

In a medium bowl, mix together the crushed tortilla chips, butter, and sugar and press into a 9 x 13-inch pan that has been prepared with nonstick cooking spray.

In a large bowl, mix together the milk, strawberries, and lime juice until well combined. Gently fold whipped topping into strawberry mixture and pour over top of crust. Freeze 4–6 hours. Let stand at room temperature 15 minutes before serving. Cut into squares and garnish with sliced fresh strawberries.

For special occasions, it is fun to make this recipe using a tart pan and decorate the top with sliced and whole strawberries.

S'MORES NACHOS

makes 4 servings

Cinnamon Crisps (p. 125)
¹/₂ cup caramel sauce
20–30 mini marshmallows
2 (1.5-ounce) chocolate candy bars, broken into pieces
1 cup graham cracker crumbs

Spread Cinnamon Crisps on a 9 x 13-inch pan or oven-proof platter. Drizzle caramel sauce and sprinkle marshmallows and chocolate pieces over top. Place on center rack of oven and broil 3–5 minutes, or until light golden brown and bubbly. Remove from oven and sprinkle with graham cracker crumbs.

UPSIDE-DOWN APPLE PIE

makes 6–8 servings

½ cup butter, melted, divided
½ cup brown sugar, divided
1 cup chopped pecans
½ cup sugar
¼ cup flour
1 teaspoon cinnamon
6 cups peeled and sliced tart apples, such as Granny Smith
1 large flour tortilla
Ice cream

Preheat oven to 350 degrees.

Prepare an 8-inch pie pan with nonstick cooking spray. Line pie pan with wax paper. In a small bowl, mix together ¼ cup butter, ¼ cup brown sugar, and pecans; spread over wax paper in bottom of pie pan. In a large bowl, combine remaining ingredients except tortilla and spread evenly in pie pan. Place tortilla over top, trimming excess around edges to make tortilla fit pie pan. Press down to remove air pockets. Cut slits in tortilla.

Bake 60–80 minutes, or until golden brown and heated through. Remove and cool 20–30 minutes. Invert onto a serving plate and remove wax paper. Serve immediately with ice cream, if desired.

MINI APPLE CHIMICHANGAS

Canola oil for frying
6 small flour tortillas
1 (19-ounce) can apple pie filling
2–3 tablespoons caramel sauce
1 cup whipped cream

Preheat oil to 375 degrees in a deep fryer or large saucepan filled no more than halfway full. Prepare tortillas by warming them slightly in the microwave. Spoon about $\frac{1}{3}$ cup of the apple filling into the center of a tortilla and roll it into a burrito; secure with toothpicks. Repeat with remaining tortillas. Fry the chimichangas until golden brown and crispy, but not hard. Drain on paper towels. To serve, top each chimichanga with caramel sauce and whipped cream.

ICE CREAM BERRY TORTILLA BOWLS

makes 6 servings

2 tablespoons cinnamon
1/2 cup sugar
6 tablespoons butter, softened
6 small flour tortillas
Ice cream
Berries, of choice

Preheat oven to 350 degrees. Spray 6 large muffin tins or 8-ounce ramekins with cooking spray and set aside.

In a small bowl, combine the cinnamon and sugar. Spread a thin layer of butter on both sides of each tortilla and sprinkle the cinnamon sugar mixture evenly on both sides. Carefully place the tortillas into the prepared muffin tins or ramekins, folding and pressing against the sides. The tortillas will stick up and out of the tins/ramekins. Place the muffin tin/ramekins on a large baking sheet and bake for 17–20 minutes, or until tortillas are golden brown and crisp. Remove the tortilla bowls and place on a wire rack to cool completely. Place on serving plates. Fill with ice cream and berries. Serve immediately.

TORTILLA CREPES SUZETTE

makes 4 servings

6 eggs
1 ½ cups half-and-half
1 teaspoon vanilla
8 large thin flour tortillas
10 tablespoons butter, divided
½ cup sugar
Juice and zest of 2 Valencia or juice oranges

Whisk the eggs, half-and-half, and vanilla in a large frying pan. One at a time, place tortillas in the egg mixture and let soak for 1 minute on each side. Place tortillas on a flat surface, such as a cutting board. Wipe out frying pan with a paper towel.

Heat frying pan to medium heat. Melt ½ tablespoon of butter in frying pan. Cook a soaked tortilla for 1–2 minutes on each side. Repeat with remaining tortillas, using ½ tablespoon of butter for each tortilla. As each tortilla is finished cooking, fold it in half and in half again, forming a triangle shape. Place 2 folded tortillas on each serving plate, and keep warm.

With an electric mixer, whip remaining butter and sugar until light and fluffy. Slowly add in the orange juice and zest while mixer is running. Drizzle the orange juice mixture over the folded crepe triangles. Serve immediately.

LEMON BERRY NACHOS

makes 4–6 servings

1 cup raspberries
1 cup water
1 cup sugar, divided
8 ounces cream cheese, softened
Juice and zest of 1 lemon
1 recipe Cinnamon Crisps (p. 125)
4 cups sliced strawberries, or berry of choice
Powdered sugar

Place raspberries, water and ½ cup sugar in a saucepan. Bring to a simmer and cook for 5 minutes, stirring frequently. Strain sauce and set aside.

In a small bowl, whisk together the cream cheese, lemon juice and zest, and remaining sugar.

Place the Cinnamon Crisps on a serving platter. Drizzle both sauces over crisps and top with fruit. Dust with powdered sugar and serve immediately.

fun treats & snacks

CHOCOLATE HAZELNUT TORTILLA SNOWFLAKES

makes 6 snowflakes

6 large, thin flour tortillas
1 cup chocolate hazelnut spread (like Nutella)
1 cup powdered sugar

Place a tortilla in the microwave for 20–30 seconds, or until softened. Remove from microwave and fold in half then fold in half again. Cut a design into folded tortilla, just like cutting a paper snowflake. Open up, place tortilla snowflake on a plate, and microwave 30 seconds. Take tortilla off the plate, wipe off any excess moisture, and let cool. Repeat this process of microwaving for 30 seconds at a time and wiping the plate until the tortilla is crisp but not brown. Repeat this process with remaining tortillas.

Place tortillas on a sheet of wax paper. Warm the hazelnut spread in microwave oven until very loose and spreadable, about 30 seconds. Using a small paintbrush, paint chocolate spread on tortillas. Dust each snowflake generously with powdered sugar.

TORTILLA CLOWN FACES

makes 6 servings

6 small flour tortillas
3 tablespoons butter
6 tablespoons cinnamon sugar
1 (8-ounce) container whipped cream cheese, softened
Sliced fruits, coconut, nuts, and chocolate chips

In a small frying pan, sauté and flip over each tortilla in ½ tablespoon butter until light golden brown and crisp on both sides. Remove, sprinkle with cinnamon sugar, and cool. Spread with cream cheese. Make a face by placing fruit, coconut, nuts, and chocolate chips over cream cheese.

TORTILLA ELEPHANT EARS

makes 8 servings

2 cups canola oil
8 small gordita-style flour tortillas
2 tablespoons cinnamon
1 cup sugar

Heat oil over medium heat in a small frying pan. Fry each tortilla in oil, turning over until light golden brown on each side. Mix together cinnamon and sugar. Spread sugar mixture on a large plate. Using tongs, remove tortilla from pan and immediately press each side of tortilla into sugar mixture. Serve warm.

Variation: Use festive holiday cookie cutters to cut holes in tortillas before frying. For Halloween cut a jack-o'-lantern face in the tortilla before frying.

BANANA SPLIT ROLL-UP

makes 1 serving

1 medium flour tortilla
2 tablespoons chocolate hazelnut spread (like Nutella)
2 tablespoons minced nuts, such as almonds or pecans
2 tablespoons minced maraschino cherries
1 medium banana, peeled

Spread tortilla with chocolate spread. Sprinkle nuts and cherries over top. Place banana on one edge of tortilla. Make small cuts on the inside curve of the banana so that it can be straightened out. Roll tortilla up, jelly-roll style.

SOUTHWEST TORTILLA PIZZAS

makes 4 pizzas

8 medium, gordita-style flour tortillas
1 (18-ounce) jar pizza sauce
2 cups grated mozzarella cheese
2 cups pizza toppings, of choice
1 cup grated Parmesan cheese

Preheat oven to 450 degrees.

Spread 3 tablespoons pizza sauce on one side of a tortilla. Press another tortilla on top. Repeat with remaining tortillas to make a total of 4 pizza crusts. Place on a wire rack on a baking sheet or directly on oven rack in oven. Bake 8 minutes. Remove from oven and press flat with a dishtowel to remove air bubbles. Turn tortillas over and bake another 2–3 minutes, or until crisp and brown. Remove from oven and press flat again.

Place on baking sheet and top with pizza sauce, mozzarella cheese, and toppings, as desired. Place in oven on center rack. Broil until toppings are hot and cheese is bubbly. Remove from oven and sprinkle with Parmesan cheese.

SLOPPY JOE TACOS

makes 4-6 servings

1 tablespoon olive oil
1 small onion, diced
3 jalapeños, seeded and diced
1 pound lean ground beef
1 (15-ounce) can diced tomatoes with green chiles
1 tablespoon Worcestershire sauce
1 tablespoon chile powder
1 tablespoon garlic powder
1 tablespoon soy sauce
1 tablespoon ground cumin
1 tablespoon smoked paprika
1 teaspoon mustard
12 corn tortillas, heated
Suggested garnishes: crumbled queso fresco cheese, thinly sliced lettuce, diced
    tomatoes, sliced radishes

Heat oil in a large frying pan over medium-high heat. Sauté onion and jalapeños until softened, about 3 minutes, stirring constantly. Add ground beef and cook until browned, breaking into small bits. Drain grease. Add remaining ingredients except tortillas and garnishes and reduce to a simmer. Cook until most of the liquid has evaporated, about 20 minutes. Serve over tortillas and top with garnishes, as desired.

PEANUT BUTTER S'MORES WRAP

makes 1 serving

1 tablespoon peanut butter
1 medium flour tortilla
1/8 cup milk chocolate chips
1/4 cup mini marshmallows

Spread peanut butter over tortilla. Sprinkle remaining ingredients over top. Microwave 45 seconds. Allow to cool 3–5 minutes. Roll jelly-roll style when cool.

Variation: Substitute grated carrots, apples, raisins, bananas, or crushed pineapple for chocolate chips and marshmallows.

CINNAMON CRISPS

makes 3-4 servings

6 large thin flour tortillas
¼ cup sugar
1 teaspoon cinnamon

Preheat oven to 400 degrees.

Lightly sprinkle tortillas with water. Combine sugar and cinnamon, and sprinkle over tortillas. Cut each tortilla into 8 wedges. Lightly spray a wire rack with oil. Place wedges in a single layer on the wire rack on a baking sheet. Bake 8–10 minutes, or until light golden brown and crisp. Serve with fruit salsa or your favorite fruit dip.

INDEX

METRIC CONVERSION CHART

volume measurements		weight measurements		temperature conversion	
U.S.	**Metric**	**U.S.**	**Metric**	**Fahrenheit**	**Celsius**
1 teaspoon	5 ml	½ ounce	15 g	250	120
1 tablespoon	15 ml	1 ounce	30 g	300	150
¼ cup	60 ml	3 ounces	90 g	325	160
⅓ cup	75 ml	4 ounces	115 g	350	180
½ cup	125 ml	8 ounces	225 g	375	190
⅔ cup	150 ml	12 ounces	350 g	400	200
¾ cup	175 ml	1 pound	450 g	425	220
1 cup	250 ml	2¼ pounds	1 kg	450	230